VOL. 41

HAL•LEONARD®

DRUM PLAY-ALONG

Rock
SONGS FOR KIDS

AUDIO ACCESS INCLUDED

Play 8 Songs with Sound-Alike Audio

PLAYBACK+
Speed • Pitch • Balance • Loop

To access audio visit:
www.halleonard.com/mylibrary

Enter Code
1394-6521-7746-1077

ISBN 978-1-4950-2836-6

HAL•LEONARD®
CORPORATION
7777 W. BLUEMOUND RD. P.O. BOX 13819 MILWAUKEE, WI 53213

Visit Hal Leonard Online at
www.halleonard.com

ROCK SONGS FOR KIDS

Play 8 Songs with Sound-Alike Audio

CONTENTS

ABC

Words and Music by Alphonso Mizell, Frederick Perren,
Deke Richards and Berry Gordy

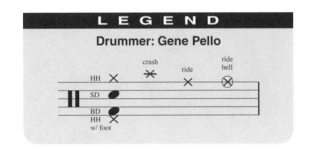

Intro
Moderately ♩ = 94

𝄋 **Verse**

2nd time, substitute Fill 1

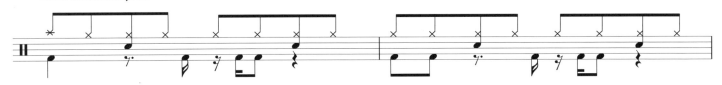

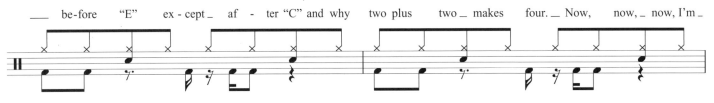

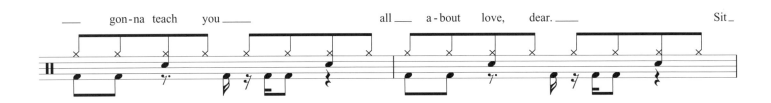

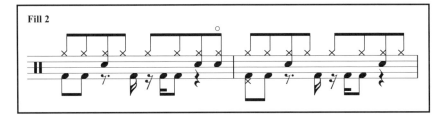

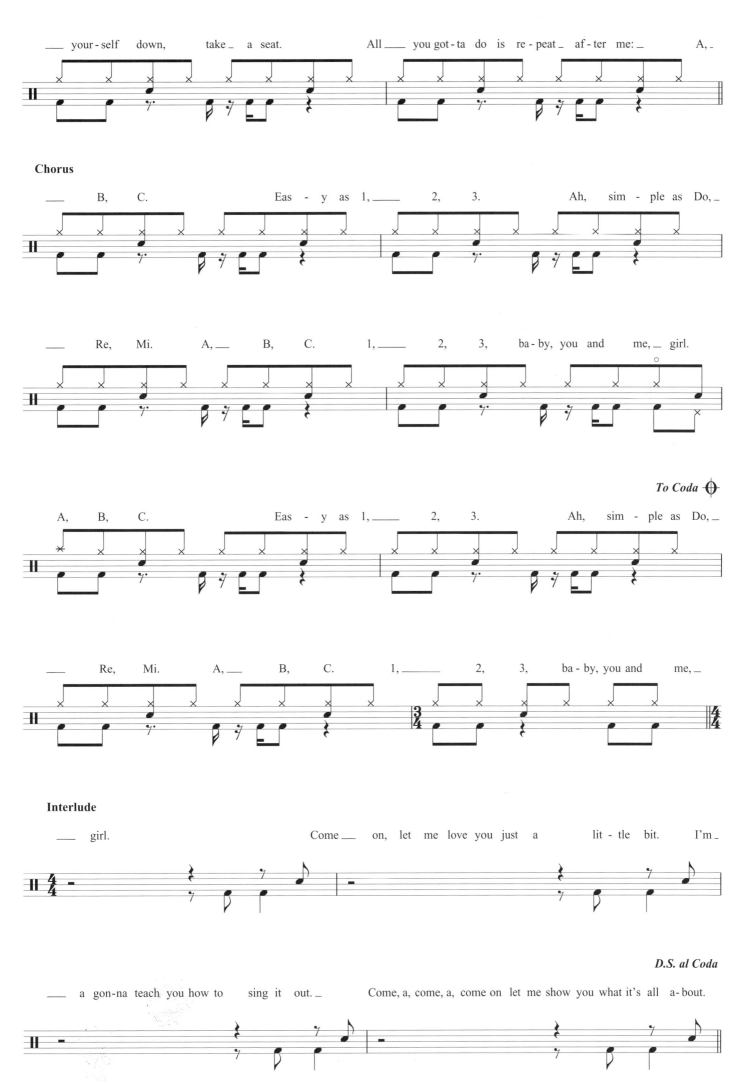

Coda

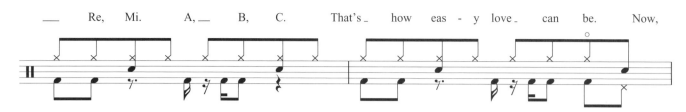

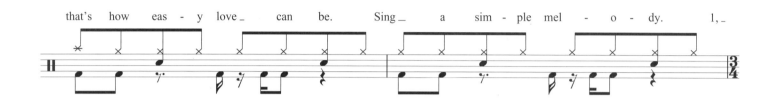

Bridge

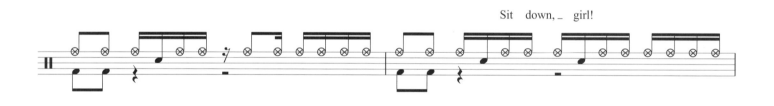

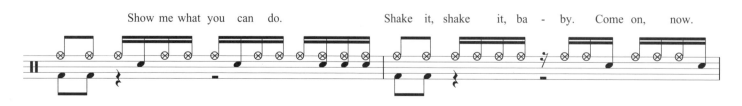

Shake it, shake it, ba - by. Oo. __ Shake it, shake it, ba - by. Ho!

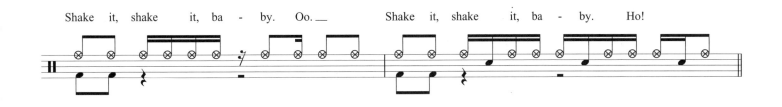

Outro-Chorus

1, 2, 3, ba - by. Oo, __ oo. A, B, C, ba - by. Na, __ na.

Do, Re, Mi, ba - by. Ow! That's how eas - y love __ can be.

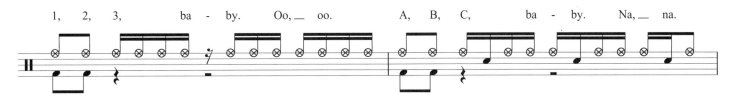

A, B, C. 1, __ 2, 3. Do, __

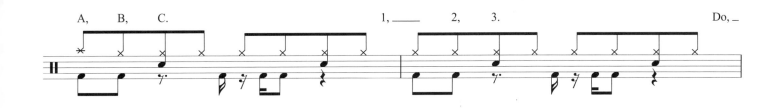

__ Re, Mi. A, __ B, C. That's __ how eas - y love __ can

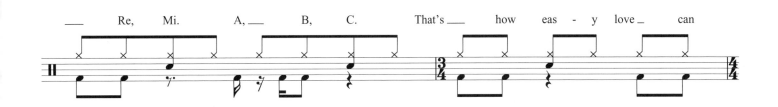

w/ Voc. ad lib.

be.

7

Begin fade

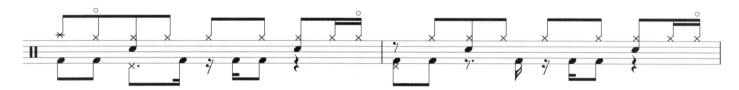

Fade out

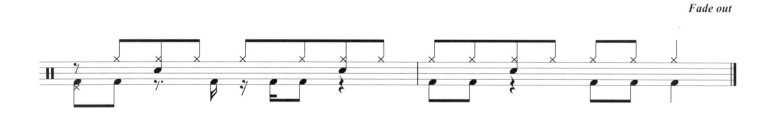

Additional Lyrics

2. Reading and writing, arithmetic,
   Are the branches on the learning tree.
   But listen, without the roots of love ev'ryday, girl,
   Your education ain't complete.
   Te-Te-Te-Teacher's gonna show you how to get an "A".
   Spell "Me", "You"; add the two.
   Listen to me, baby. That's all you gotta do.

I Love Rock 'N Roll

Words and Music by Alan Merrill and Jake Hooker

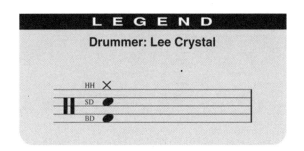

Chorus

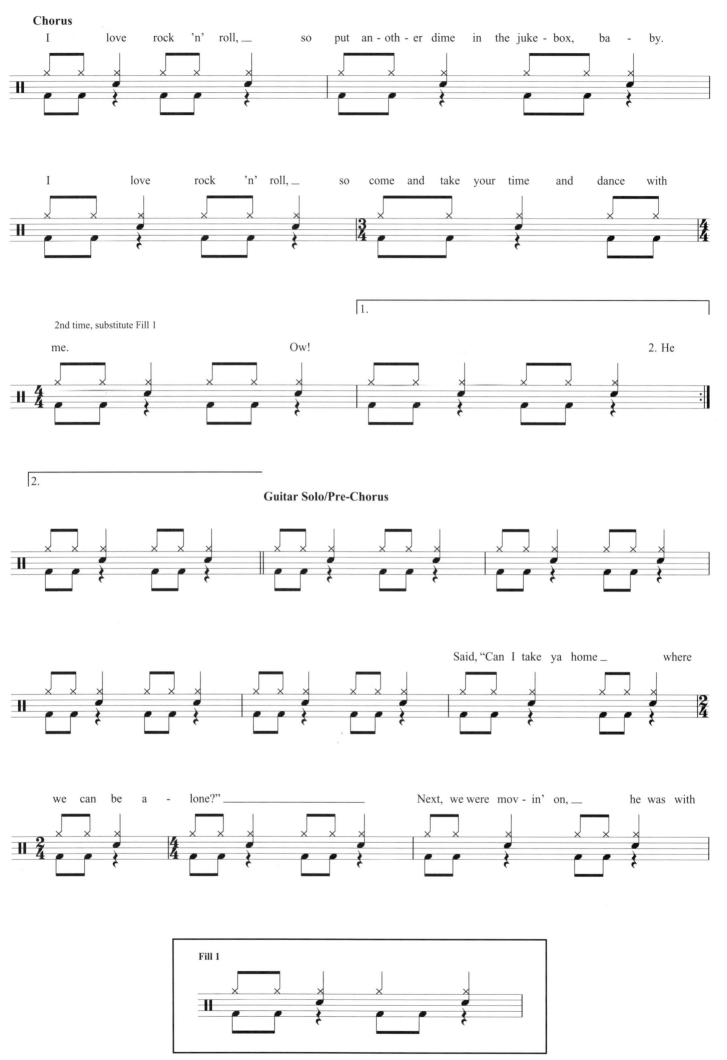

I love rock 'n' roll, ___ so put an-oth-er dime in the juke - box, ba - by.

I love rock 'n' roll, ___ so come and take your time and dance with

2nd time, substitute Fill 1

me.   Ow!   2. He

1.

2.

Guitar Solo/Pre-Chorus

Said, "Can I take ya home ___ where

we can be a - lone?" _____ Next, we were mov - in' on, ___ he was with

Fill 1

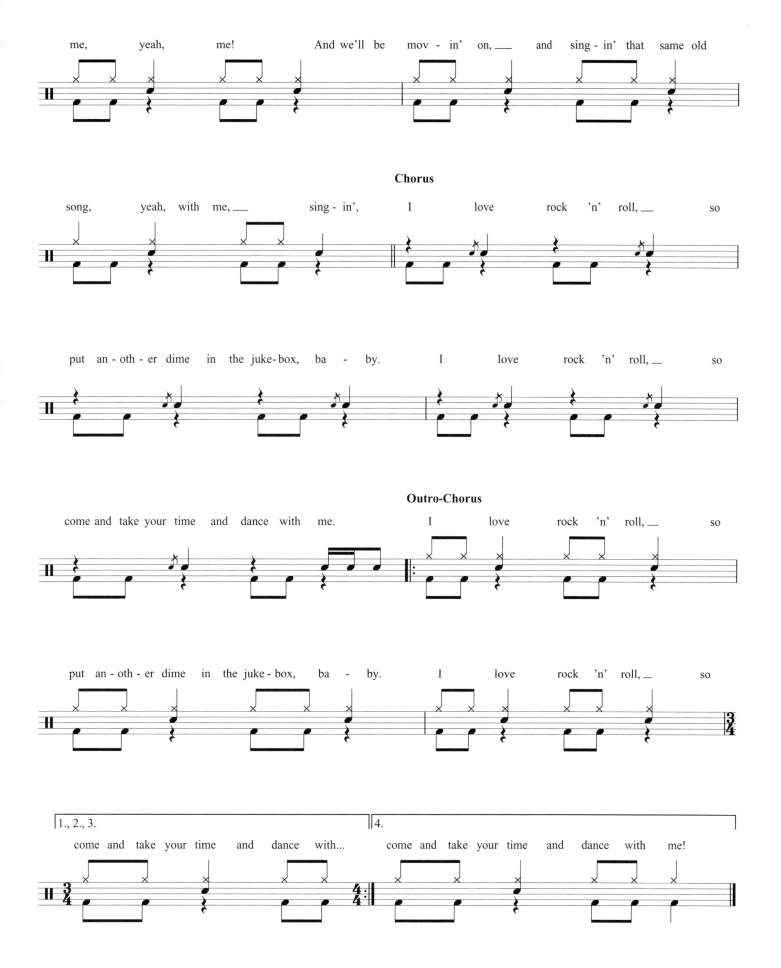

Additional Lyrics

2. He smiled, so I got up and asked for his name.
"That don't matter," he said, "'cause it's all the same."
I said, "Can I take ya home where we can be alone?"
And next, we were movin' on, he was with me, yeah, me!
Next, we were movin' on, he was with me, yeah, me, singin',...

Happy

from DESPICABLE ME 2

Words and Music by Pharrell Williams

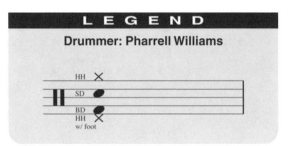

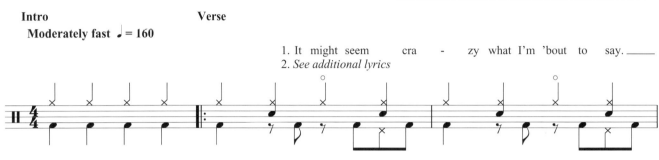

Intro

Moderately fast ♩ = 160

Verse

1. It might seem cra - zy what I'm 'bout to say. ___
2. *See additional lyrics*

Sun - shine, ___ she's here; ___

___ you can take a break. ___   I'm a

hot ___ air bal - loon ___ that could go to space. ___

With the air, ___ like I don't care, ___ ba - by, by the way.

Chorus

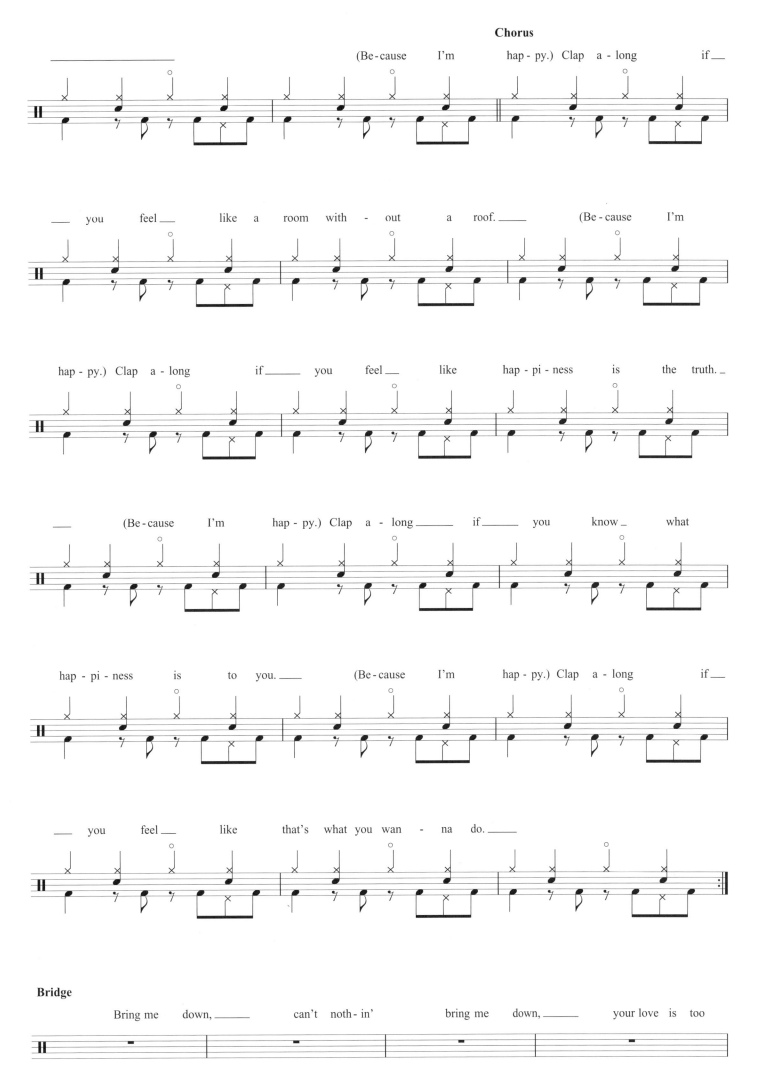

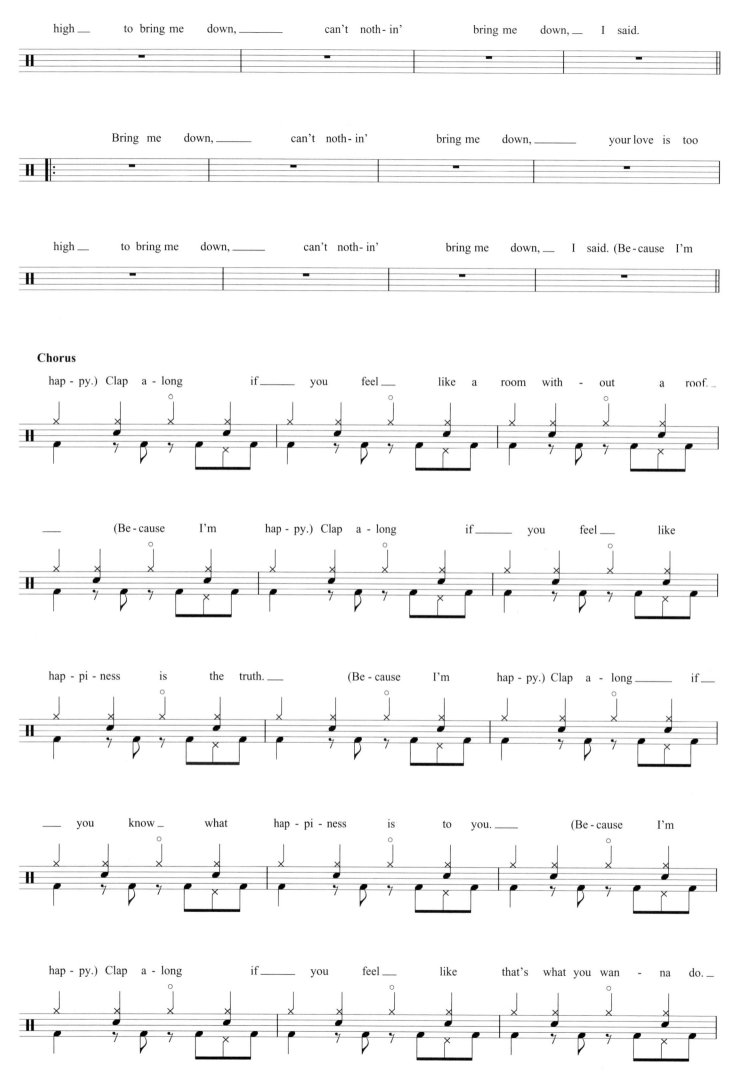

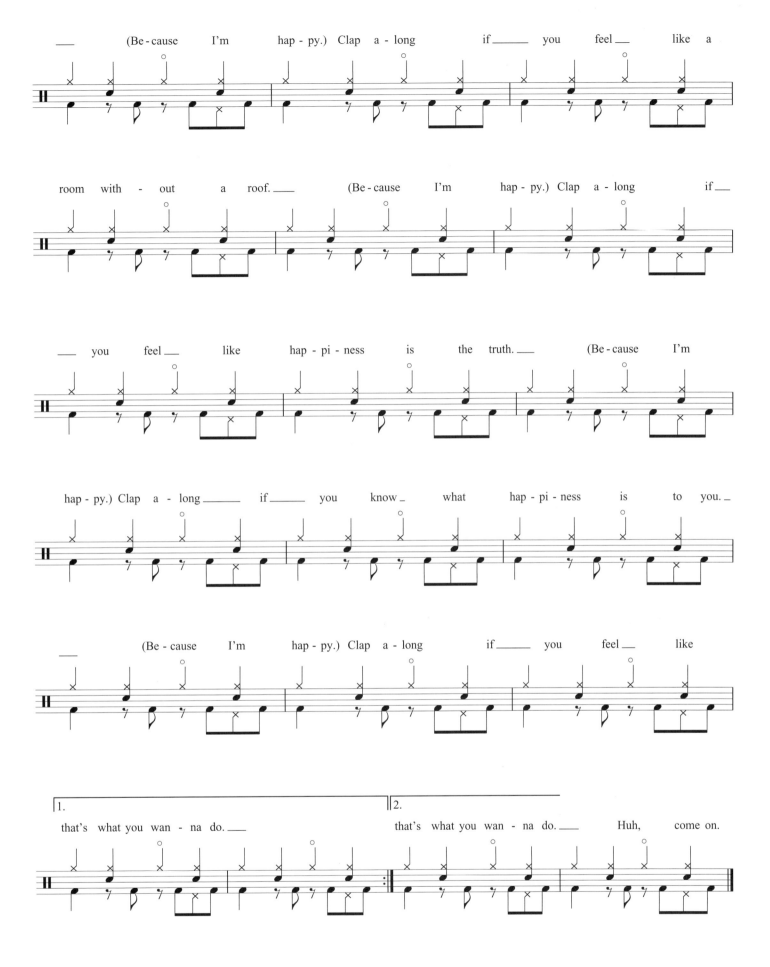

Additional Lyrics

2. Here come bad news, talkin' this and that.
Well, gimme all you got and don't hold it back.
Well, I should prob'ly warn you, I'll be just fine.
No offense to you, don't waste your time. Here's why:

I'm a Believer

Words and Music by Neil Diamond

Intro
Moderately fast ♩ = 160

Verse

1. I thought love was on - ly true ___ in fair - y tales,

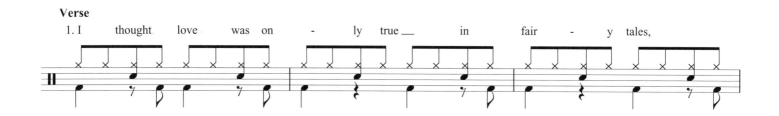

meant for some-one else ___ but not for me. ___

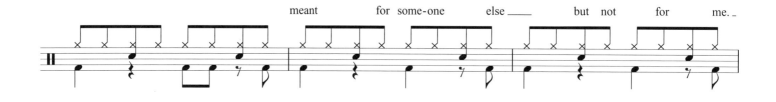

Pre-Chorus

Love was out to get ___ me. That's the way it seemed. ___

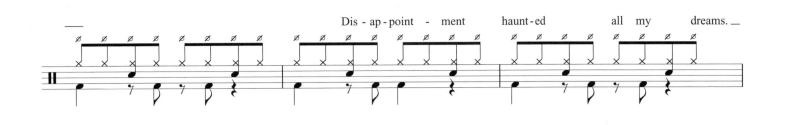

Dis - ap - point - ment haunt-ed all my dreams. __

Then I saw her face; __

𝄋 Chorus

now I'm __ a be - liev - er!

Not a trace _____ of doubt _ in my mind. __

2nd time, substitute Fill 1
3rd time, substitute Fill 2

I'm in love,

To Coda 2

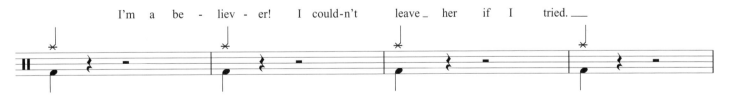

I'm a be - liev - er! I could-n't leave _ her if I tried. __

Fill 1

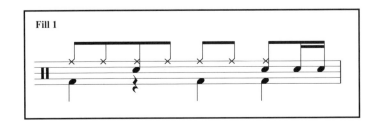

Fill 2

To Coda 1

Verse

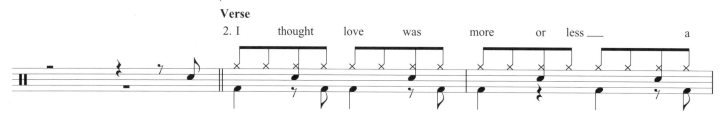

2. I thought love was more or less ___ a

giv - in' thing. ___ Seems the more I gave, ___

___ the less I got. ___

Pre-Chorus

What's the use in try - in'? All you get is pain. ___

___ When I need - ed sun - shine, I got rain. ___

D.S. al Coda 1

Then I saw her face; ___

18

⊕ Coda 1

Keyboard Solo

Ah, _____

Pre-Chorus

___ love was out to get ___ me.   Now, that's the way it seemed. ___

___   Dis - ap - point - ment   haunt-ed   all my   dreams. ___

D.S. al Coda 2

___   Then   I   saw   her   face; ___

⊕ Coda 2

Yes, I saw her face; _____ now I'm _ a be-liev-

- er! Well, not _____ a trace _

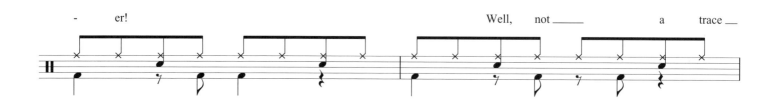

_____ of doubt _ in my _ mind. _

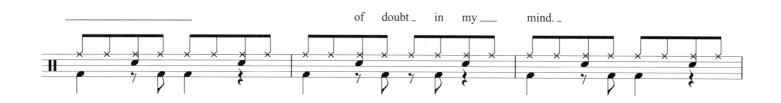

Said I'm _ a be - liev - er, yeah, _ yeah, _ yeah, _ yeah, _ yeah, _ yeah. _____

Begin fade

_____ Said I'm _ a be - liev - er, yeah.

Fade out

I said I'm _ a be - liev - er, yeah, _____ yeah, _____ oh. _____

Let's Get It Started

Words and Music by Will Adams, Allan Pineda, Jaime Gomez,
Michael Fratantuno, George Pajon Jr. and Terence Yoshiaki Graves

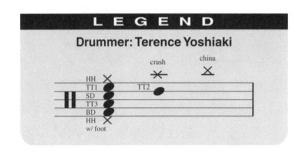

Intro
Moderately ♩ = 105

And the bass keeps run-nin', run-nin' and run-nin', run-nin' and

run-nin', run-nin' and run-nin', run-nin' and run-nin', run-nin' and run-nin', run-nin' and

Verse

run-nin', run-nin' and run-nin', run-nin' and... 1. In this con-text there's no dis-re-spect,

so when I bust _ my rhymes, you break _ your necks. We've got five min-utes for us to dis-con-nect

from all in-tel-lect and let the rhy-thm af-fect. To lose the in-hi-bi-tion, fol-low your in-tu-i-tion.

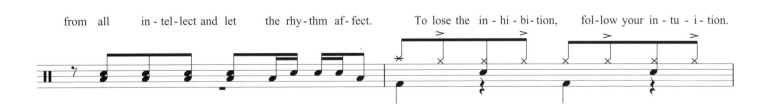

Verse

Pre-Chorus

Chorus

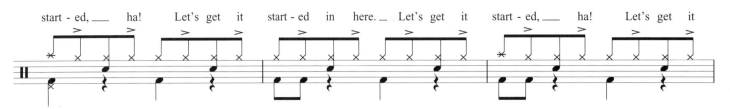

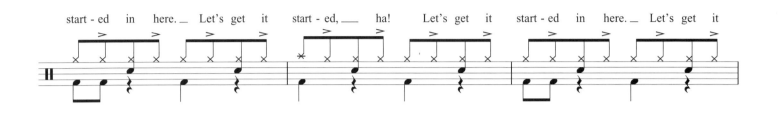

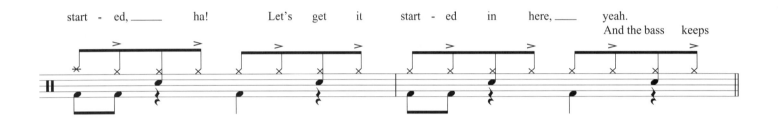

Interlude

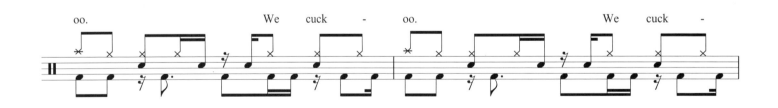

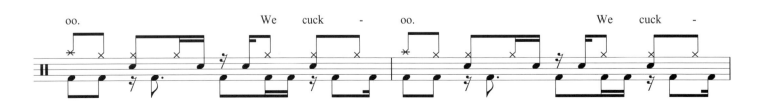

oo.　　　　　　We cuck - 　oo.

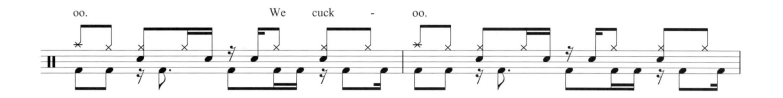

Ya, ya, ya, ya, ya, ya, ya, ya, ya, ya, ya, ya, ya, ya, ya,

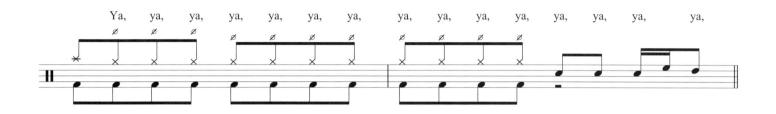

Bridge

ya. Let's get ill, that's the deal. __ At the gate, we'll bring the bud, top drill. (Just)

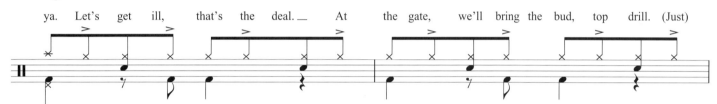

lose your mind, this is the time, __ y'all guessed this ill just to bang your spine. __ (Just)

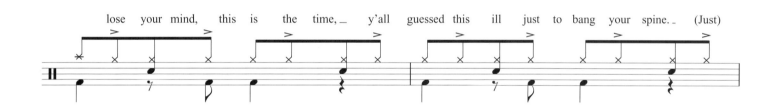

bob your head like me, Ap - ple __ Dee, up in - side your club or in your Bent - ley.

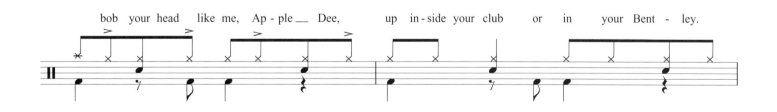

Get mess - y, loud and sick, your mind past nor - mal on an - oth - er head - trip. So,

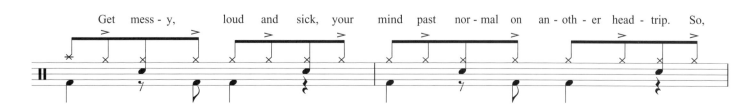

come then now, do not cor - rect ___ it, let's get ig - 'nant, let's get hec - tic.

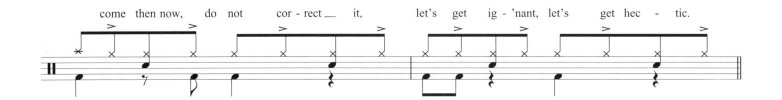

Pre-Chorus

Ev - 'ry-bod - y, ev - 'ry-bod - y just get ___ in - to it and get ___ stu -

pid. Get it start - ed, get it start - ed, get it start - ed. Let's get it

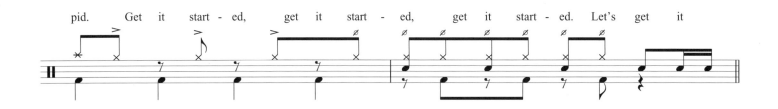

Chorus

start - ed, ___ ha! Let's get it start - ed in here. ___ Let's get it

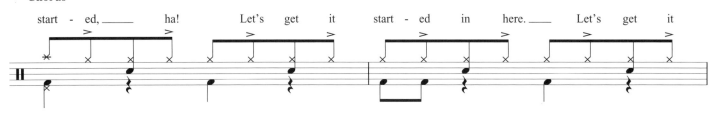

start - ed, ___ ha! Let's get it start - ed in here. ___ Let's get it

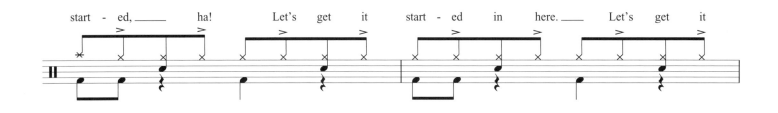

start - ed, ___ ha! Let's get it start - ed in here. ___ Let's get it

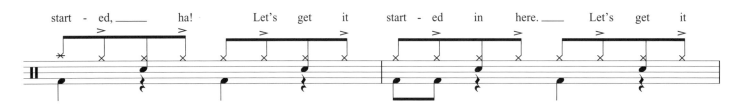

start - ed, _____ ha! Let's get it start - ed in here. _____ We cuck -

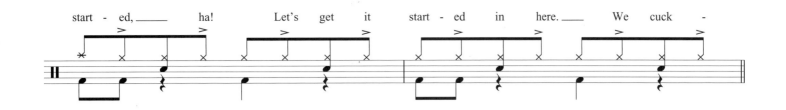

Outro

oo. We cuck - oo. We cuck -

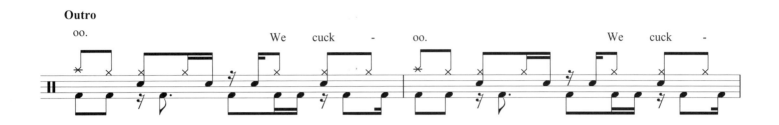

oo. We cuck - oo. We cuck -

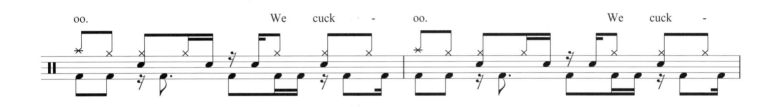

oo. We cuck - oo. Come on ___ and sing.
Run - nin', run - nin' and run - nin', run - nin' and run - nin', run - nin' and run - nin', run - nin' and...

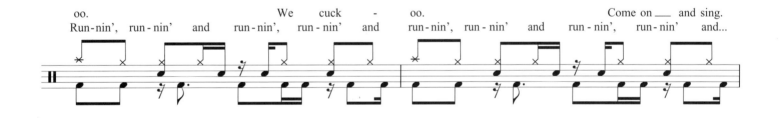

Ya, ya, ya, ya, ya, ya, ya, ya, ya, ya, ya, ya, ya, ya, ya,

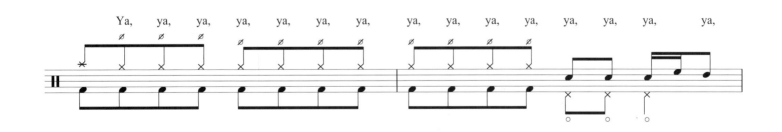

Repeat and fade

ya.

Surfin' U.S.A.

Words and Music by Chuck Berry

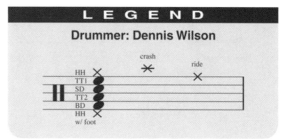

Intro
Moderately fast ♩ = 160

1.If ev - 'ry - bod - y had an

Verse

o - cean — a - cross the U. S. A., ___

2. *See additional lyrics*

then ev - 'ry - bod - y'd be surf - in' — like Cal - i - forn - i - a. —

___ You'd see 'em wear - ing their bag - gies, —

Hua - ra - chi san - dals, too. — A bush - y, bush - y blonde

hair - do, — surf - in' U. S. A. —

Chorus

Organ/Guitar Solo

Ev - 'ry - bod - y's gone

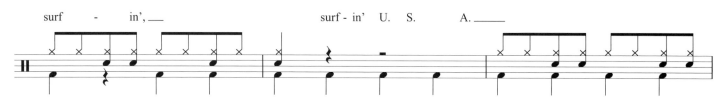

Outro

surf - in', ___   surf - in' U. S.   A. _____

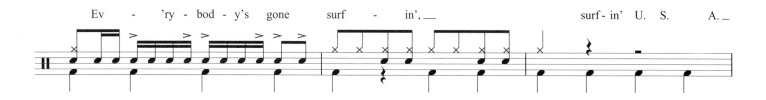

Ev - 'ry - bod - y's gone   surf - in', ___   surf - in' U. S.   A. _

Begin fade

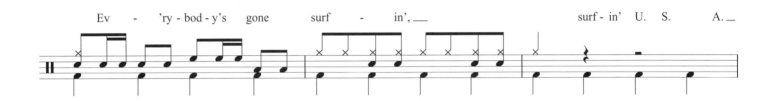

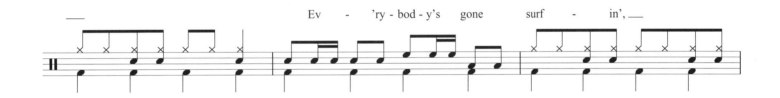

Fade out

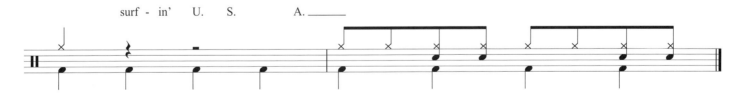

Additional Lyrics

2. We'll all be planning out a route we're gonna take real soon.
   We're waxin' down our surfboards; we can't wait for June.
   We'll all be gone for the summer; we're on safari to stay.
   Tell the teacher we're surfin', surfin' U.S.A.

Chorus At Haggerty's and Swami's, Pacific Palisades.
   San Onofre and Sunset, Redondo Beach, L.A.
   All over La Jolla; at Waiamea Bay.
   Ev'rybody's gone surfin', surfin' U.S.A.

Low Rider

Words and Music by Sylvester Allen, Harold R. Brown,
Morris Dickerson, Jerry Goldstein, Leroy Jordan,
Lee Oskar, Charles W. Miller and Howard Scott

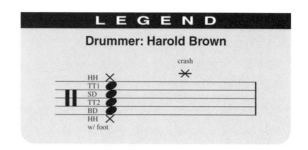

Intro

Moderately fast Rock ♩ = 138

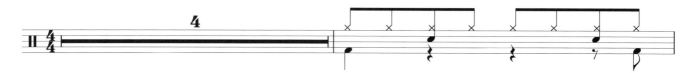

Verse

1. All   my   friends   know the low   rid - er.

The low   rid -   er   is a lit - tle

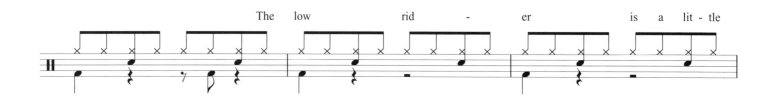

high - er.   **Chorus**

Verse

2. Low   rid -

er   drives a lit - tle slow - er.

Low   rid -   er,   he's a real   go - er.

Chorus

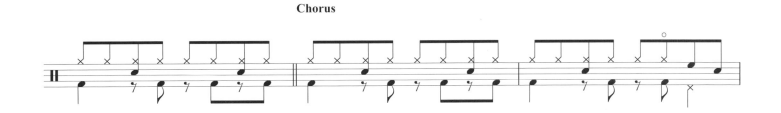

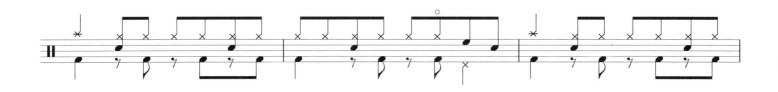

Verse

3. Low   rid   -   er   knows   ev - 'ry

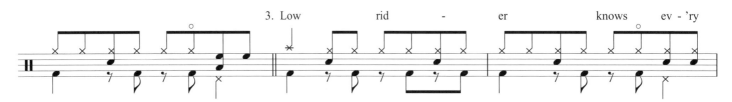

street,   yeah.   Low   rid -

er   is   the   one   to   meet,   yeah.

Chorus

Verse

4. Low   rid -

er   don't   use   no   gas   now.

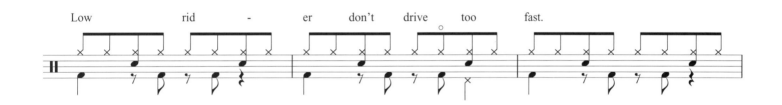

Low   rid -   er   don't   drive   too   fast.

Chorus

Outro

Take a lit - tle trip,   take a lit - tle trip,   take a lit - tle trip   and see.

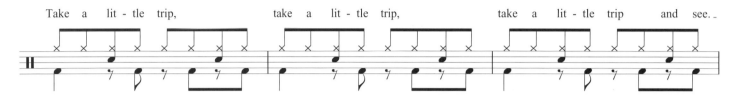

Take a lit - tle trip,   take a lit - tle trip,

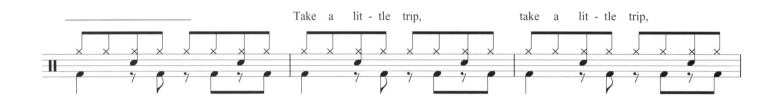

take a lit - tle trip   with me.

Repeat and fade

36

Yellow Submarine

Words and Music by John Lennon and Paul McCartney

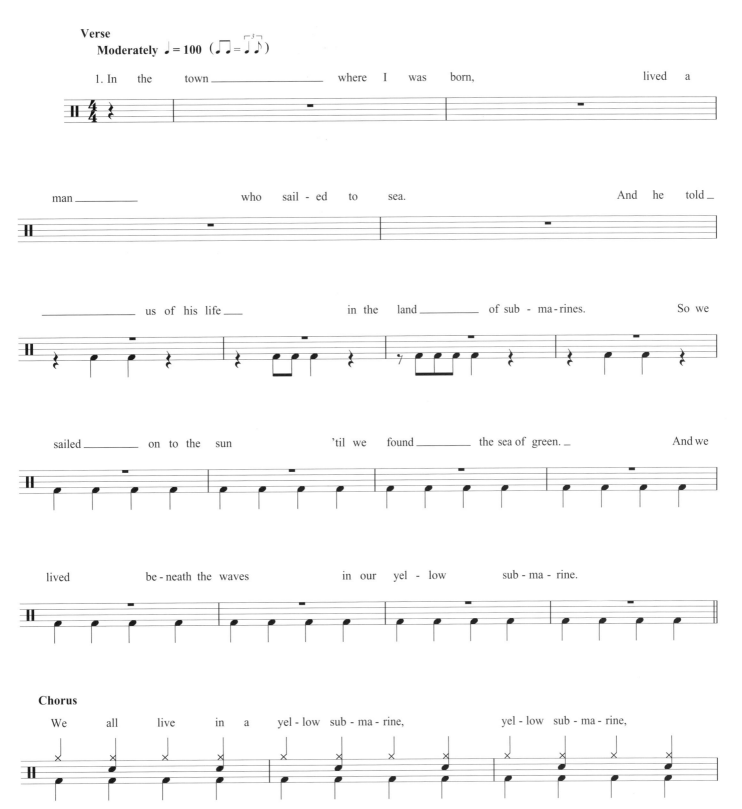

yel - low sub - ma - rine.   We   all   live   in a   yel - low sub - ma - rine,

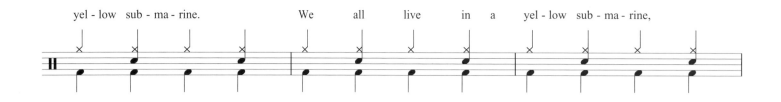

Verse

yel - low sub - ma - rine,   yel - low sub - ma - rine. 2. And our friends _____ are all a -

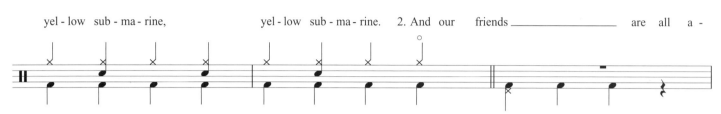

board,   man - y more of them   live next door.   And the

band _____ be - gins to ____ play.

Chorus

We   all   live   in a   yel - low sub - ma - rine,   yel - low sub - ma - rine,

yel - low sub - ma - rine.   We   all   live   in a   yel - low sub - ma - rine,

Interlude

yel - low sub - ma - rine,   yel - low sub - ma - rine.

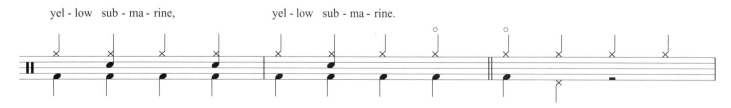

3. As we

Verse

live _____ a life of ease, ev - 'ry one of us has all we

need. Sky of blue _____ and sea of green, in our

Outro-Chorus

yel - low sub - ma - rine. We all live in a

yel - low sub - ma - rine, a yel - low sub - ma - rine, yel - low sub - ma - rine.

We all live in a yel - low sub - ma - rine, a

Repeat and fade

yel - low sub - ma - rine, yel - low sub - ma - rine.

DRUM PLAY-ALONG

AUDIO ACCESS INCLUDED

The Drum Play-Along™ Series will help you play your favorite songs quickly and easily! Just follow the drum notation, listen to the audio to hear how the drums should sound, and then play-along using the separate backing tracks. The lyrics are also included for reference. The audio files are enhanced so you can adjust the recording to any tempo without changing pitch!

1. Pop/Rock
00699742.....................................$14.99

2. Classic Rock
00699741.....................................$16.99

3. Hard Rock
00699743.....................................$17.99

4. Modern Rock
00699744.....................................$19.99

5. Funk
00699745.....................................$16.99

6. '90s Rock
00699746.....................................$17.99

7. Punk Rock
00699747.....................................$14.99

8. '80s Rock
00699832.....................................$16.99

9. Cover Band Hits
00211599.....................................$16.99

10. blink-182
00699834.....................................$19.99

11. Jimi Hendrix Experience: Smash Hits
00699835.....................................$19.99

12. The Police
00700268.....................................$16.99

13. Steely Dan
00700202.....................................$17.99

15. The Beatles
00256656.....................................$17.99

16. Blues
00700272.....................................$17.99

17. Nirvana
00700273.....................................$16.99

18. Motown
00700274.....................................$16.99

19. Rock Band: Modern Rock Edition
00700707.....................................$17.99

20. Rock Band: Classic Rock Edition
00700708.....................................$14.95

21. Weezer
00700959.....................................$14.99

22. Black Sabbath
00701190.....................................$17.99

23. The Who
00701191.....................................$19.99

24. Pink Floyd – Dark Side of the Moon
00701612.....................................$17.99

25. Bob Marley
00701703.....................................$19.99

26. Aerosmith
00701887.....................................$19.99

27. Modern Worship
00701921.....................................$16.99

28. Avenged Sevenfold
00702388.....................................$19.99

29. Queen
00702389.....................................$17.99

30. Dream Theater
00111942.....................................$24.99

31. Red Hot Chili Peppers
00702992.....................................$19.99

32. Songs for Beginners
00704204.....................................$15.99

33. James Brown
00117422.....................................$17.99

34. U2
00124470.....................................$17.99

35. Buddy Rich
00124640.....................................$19.99

36. Wipe Out & 7 Other Fun Songs
00125341.....................................$17.99

37. Slayer
00139861.....................................$17.99

38. Eagles
00143920.....................................$17.99

39. Kiss
00143937.....................................$16.99

40. Stevie Ray Vaughan
00146155.....................................$16.99

41. Rock Songs for Kids
00148113.....................................$15.99

42. Easy Rock Songs
00148143.....................................$15.99

45. Bon Jovi
00200891.....................................$17.99

46. Mötley Crüe
00200892.....................................$16.99

47. Metallica: 1983-1988
00234340.....................................$19.99

48. Metallica: 1991-2016
00234341.....................................$19.99

49. Top Rock Hits
00256655.....................................$16.99

51. Deep Purple
00278400.....................................$16.99

52. More Songs for Beginners
00278403.....................................$14.99

53. Pop Songs for Kids
00298650.....................................$15.99

HAL•LEONARD®

Visit Hal Leonard Online at
www.halleonard.com

Prices, contents and availability subject to change without notice and may vary outside the US.